SPAIN
AND THE SPANISH

ED NEEDHAM

FRANKLIN WATTS
LONDON • SYDNEY

This edition printed in 2001

© Aladdin Books Ltd 1993

Designed and produced by
Aladdin Books Ltd
28 Percy Street
London W1P 0LD

914.6

First published in
Great Britain in 1993 by
Watts Books
96 Leonard Street
London EC2A 4XD

ISBN 0-7496-3882-6

A CIP catalogue record for this book is
available from the British Library.

Printed in U.A.E.

Design   David West Children's
                Book Design
Designer   Flick
Editors   Suzanne Melia
                Mark Jackson
Picture research Emma Krikler
Illustrators   David Burroughs
                Peter Kesteven

The author, Ed Needham, has lived in
Barcelona, where he worked as a translator
and journalist. He has also worked for the
Barcelona Olympic Organising Committee.

The consultant, Maria Hernandez, was
born in Spain and now lives in Britain,
where she teaches Spanish.

INTRODUCTION

Spain is a country of many contrasts,
exotic yet European. It is often seen as a
passionate, mysterious country – a land of
art, ancient history, culture and religion
whose influences touch almost every
corner of the globe. Spain has been the
inspiration for many artists and writers
with its heroes, castles, matadors and
fiestas. Today, Spain is an ambitious,
young democracy – a member of the
EU determined to be as economically
successful as its European neighbours.
This book offers an insight into Spain
and the Spanish people, and includes
information about geography, language
and literature, science and maths,
history and the arts.

Geography
The symbol of the planet Earth
indicates where
geographical facts and
activities are examined in
this book. These sections
include a look at the 17
different regions that
make up Spain.

Language and literature
An open book is the sign for
activities and information
about language and literature.
These sections discuss what is
sometimes thought of as the
"first novel", Don Quixote, and
looks at Spain's other 3 official
languages apart from Spanish.

Science, technology and maths

The microscope symbol shows where a science or maths subject is included. These sections include a look at the amazing Roman architecture that can be seen at the aqueduct in Segovia and discusses the wildlife of the Doñana wetlands.

History

The sign of the scroll and hourglass indicates where historical information is given. These sections include a look at the historical city of Toledo and its traditional steel and armour production.

Social history

The symbol of the family shows where information about social history is given. These sections provide an insight into the Spanish way of life today, as well as describing religious beliefs, traditional festivals and customs.

Arts, crafts and music

The symbol showing a sheet of music and art tools signals where information on arts, crafts or music is included. Spain has produced many famous composers and artists, some of whom are discussed.

CONTENTS

INTRODUCTION TO SPAIN

Spain is the second largest country in Western Europe, and shares the Iberian peninsula with Portugal. Its mountains and plains, lush green valleys and barren wastelands make it one of Europe's most varied countries. Spain became a single country in 1492, and the effects of its exploration and colonisation have spread Spanish influence worldwide. Spain has a population of over 39 million, and covers an area of 504,750 km². The Balearic Islands in the Mediterranean, the Canaries in the Atlantic and the North African enclaves of Ceuta and Melilla are also part of Spain.

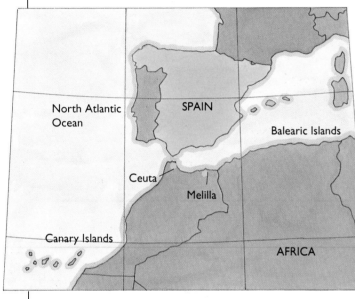

Speaking Spanish

Obviously, just about everyone in Spain speaks Spanish, which became the country's official language in the late 15th century. Spain, however, has three other official languages. Basque, or Euskera, is spoken in the Basque Country and Navarra. Catalán is the language of Catalonia, and Gallego is spoken in Galicia. People in these regions are often bilingual, and it is common for television broadcasts, newspapers and education to be in these regional languages as well. There are many regional dialects too. Some, such as Valenciano in Valencia, and Mallorquín in the Balearic islands, are widely spoken; others survive in rural areas and are spoken by very few people.

In the last 100 years, Spain has been a republic, a monarchy, a military dictatorship and a monarchy again. Juan Carlos I is the current king. His role in Spain's return to democracy has made him a popular monarch, unlike many previous Bourbon kings.

Bullfighting has been a feature of Spanish life for over 600 years. It has left its mark on painting, sculpture, music, dance and literature. The great Pedro Romero (left) is considered the father of modern bullfighting.

Latin America

Spain colonised most of Latin America after Europeans first travelled there in 1492. Its language, religion and customs were spread first by the *conquistadores* (conquerors), then by the settlers who started arriving in the mid-16th century in search of a better life. Spain still has close links with the continent. Apart from Brazil, where the people speak Portuguese, Spanish is spoken throughout Latin America. There are an estimated 330 million Spanish speakers worldwide.

Flamenco and Folk Dancing

There are many types of music and dance in Spain. Folk festivals throughout the year bring out costumed dancers like the girl below. Flamenco has its origin in the 18th century in Andalusia, when gypsies called each other *Flamencos*. It is a mournful style of singing, often accompanied by guitar music and dancing. In the dance, the men's steps are intricate, with lots of heel and toe clicking, while the women's dance depends on the grace of the hands and body. They may play *castanets* in time to the music.

From the cafés and bars of the big cities, to the huge, rolling plateau of the Meseta, Spain is a country of amazing contrasts.

The coat of arms

The Spanish flag is red and yellow, and bears the national coat of arms, which illustrates the union between the old kingdoms of Castile, León, Aragón and Granada.

ORIGINS TO GOLDEN AGE

The Iberian peninsula, which takes its name from the river Ebro, has been settled at various times by Greeks, Romans, Germanic tribes and Arabs. The Arabs, or Moors, invaded in 711 and remained for almost eight centuries, until they were driven out in 1492 by the Catholic Monarchs, Ferdinand and Isabella. Under their reign, Spain became a single country, the Americas were discovered and Spain's *Siglo de Oro*, or Golden Age, began. From 1516 to 1700, Spain was ruled by the Hapsburgs.

Hillside caves

Neanderthal man arrived in Spain as far back as half a million years ago. In 1879, scientist Don Marcelino de Sautuola and his young daughter discovered cave paintings of horses, bison, boars and stags at Altamira, Cantabria. Settlers from 15,000 years ago had painted them, perhaps to let other prehistoric people know which animals populated the area.

El Cid's real name was Rodrigo Diaz. He was finally defeated by the Moors at Cuenca and he died in 1099.

Date chart

1000 BC	Phoenicians invaded from an area that is Lebanon today.
600s BC	Greeks arrive.
200s BC	Roman invasion.
300s AD	Christianity arrives.
400s AD	Germanic tribes invade.
711-718	Moors (Muslims) conquer almost all of Spain.
1200s	Christians regain control of Castile and León.
1469	Ferdinand II of Aragón marries Isabella of Castile.
1492	Columbus reaches America.
1492	Last Muslim kingdom conquered (Granada).
1588	Armada defeated in English Channel.
1655	Philip IV dies.

The Arab legacy

Under the Moors, who had a more advanced culture than most of medieval Europe, trade and crafts flourished. Their silk, brocades, leather and jewellery were prized throughout Europe. They brought new sciences such as astrology and medicine, and new farming methods which made the land prosper. They left many fine mosques and beautiful, fortified palaces like the Alhambra in Granada.

Roman Aqueduct

The Romans were great engineers, and constructed spectacular buildings like this aqueduct north of Pamplona. The Roman aqueduct at Segovia stands 39 metres high and carried water until the 1960s. After more than 17 centuries of use, however, recent pollution and vibration caused by traffic beneath it have made it start to crumble.

Ferdinand of Aragón and Isabella of Castile married in 1469, and united their kingdoms in 1479 to form the basis of modern Spain. They finished the *Reconquista*, in which the Arabs were driven out of Spain. Earlier, the famous El Cid had participated in these battles. He fought for both sides at various times, becoming one of Spain's national heroes. The Arabs were finally defeated at Granada in 1492.

Ferdinand and Isabella

El Siglo de Oro

The 16th and 17th centuries became known as Spain's *Siglo de Oro*, or Golden Age. In spite of numerous costly wars, fresh ideas poured in from abroad, stimulated by new experiences and enthusiasm from foreign adventures. This period produced some of Spain's finest painters and writers. Diego Velázquez (1599-1660) was court painter to Philip IV, and many Spaniards consider that his portraits and still lifes make him the greatest artist ever. Amongst his most famous pictures are *Maids of Honour*, *The Tapestry Weavers* and *Venus and Cupid*. Another important painter of the period was El Greco (1541-1614), born in Crete. His masterpiece is the *Burial of Count Orgaz* (below). During this period Miguel de Cervantes wrote the novel *Don Quixote* (see page 17) and playwright Pedro Calderón de la Barca wrote the famous play *Life Is A Dream*.

The Armada

Spain was the strongest naval power in the 16th century. Philip II sent his "Invincible Armada" (armada means navy) of 130 ships and 27,000 men to invade England in 1588, partly because English piracy annoyed him and because he wanted to re-establish Roman Catholicism there. The English Navy under Lord Howard and Sir Francis Drake was lighter and better equipped, and broke up the Armada using fire ships. The Spanish were forced home around the tip of Scotland. Only 61 ships survived, and Spain's maritime prestige was never regained.

Bourbons to EU

The French Bourbons came to the Spanish throne when Philip V was crowned in 1700. They were briefly ousted in 1808 when Napoléon invaded and made his brother Joseph king. The Peninsular War followed, and the French were finally expelled with the help of the English and Portuguese. More squabbling over the throne followed as Ferdinand VII's daughter, Isabella II, was crowned in 1833. Don Carlos, Ferdinand's brother, felt he should be king. His supporters were called Carlists, and there were uprisings in 1834-39 and 1872-76.

The current king's grandfather, Alfonso XIII, became king in 1886 and abdicated in 1931 when the people voted for a republic. Civil war broke out five years later between left-wing Republicans and right-wing Nationalists, followed by the military dictatorship of General Franco. This ended on his death in 1975, and democracy was restored, along with another Bourbon king, the present monarch, Juan Carlos I.

Don Carlos (left) felt that he should be king instead of Isabella II. Alfonso XIII (above) became king in 1886.

War of Spanish Succession

Spain's last Hapsburg king, Charles II, had no children, and to stop French attacks on Spain, he decided to name Philip, the grandson of Louis XIV of France, as his heir. Philip V, therefore, became the first Bourbon king of Spain. The idea of a French prince ruling Spain horrified the other European powers, and ultimately caused the War of the Spanish Succession (1701-14). This war saw Spain lose all its European territories. These included Belgium, Luxembourg, Milan, Sardinia and Naples. Spain also lost Gibraltar and Minorca to the British. The war meant that the end of Spanish power in Europe had come, after two whole centuries as a major force.

Dictatorship

General Francisco Franco's victory in Spain's Civil War in 1939, led to nearly forty years of military dictatorship. The post-war years were a harsh time. There was fierce political repression and famine, which meant a flourishing black market, rural misery and a flight from the country to the towns. The country's recovery was complicated by the destruction caused by the Civil War, and the world turned its back on Spain. Although Franco supported Nazi Germany, Spain did not participate in World War II.

Lorca

One of Spain's most brilliant poets and playwrights, was Federico García Lorca (1898-1936). Lorca was killed in the Spanish Civil War. His famous plays are *Blood Wedding* (1933), *Yerma* (1934) and *The House of Bernarda Alba* (1936).

Date chart

1700	Philip V becomes king.
1701-1714	War of the Spanish Succession
1808	Napoléon installs his brother Joseph as king of Spain, but Bourbons restored by 1814.
1898	Spanish-American War: Spain loses Cuba, Guam, Puerto Rico, Philippines.
1931	Alfonso XIII abdicates.
1936	Spanish Civil War begins.
1939	Military dictatorship begins.
1975	Franco dies, Juan Carlos I restores democracy.
1977	First general elections held.
1986	Spain joins the European Union (EU).
1992	Olympics held in Barcelona.
1993	Spain signs Maastricht Treaty.

Civil War

The Spanish Civil War began on July 17, 1936, when a group of Nationalist rebels led by General Franco rose against the elected Republican government. Neither side was strong enough to win alone, and the Nationalists received help from the fascist governments in Italy and Germany, while the Republicans were assisted by the Soviet Union. Three years of bloody warfare left an estimated 500,000 people dead, with many more killed by disease, malnutrition and starvation. After the Nationalist victory, a lot of Republicans fled into exile, while many who remained were imprisoned or executed. Just over 50 years later, as the world's eyes focused on the Olympic games in Barcelona, little evidence of Spain's bloody past remained.

WORLD INFLUENCE

The accidental discovery of the New World by Christopher Columbus in 1492 made Spain rich and strong. Driven on by the search for gold and silver to send back home, other explorers, who became known as *conquistadores* (see page 11), plundered and destroyed entire civilisations. Within 60 years, the Spanish Empire extended from what is now the southern United States, to central Chile and Argentina, and Spain became a world power with enough wealth to finance wars in Europe.

Columbus

Christopher Columbus (Cristobal Colón) was probably born in Genoa, Italy. He left Spain in 1492 in three tiny ships in search of a western trade route to the Far East. After sailing into the unknown for three months he reached the Bahamas, then Cuba, which he thought was probably part of Japan or China. After making three further voyages, in which he reached mainland South America, he died a poor, sick and broken man.

New world of food

Along with the boatloads of plunder from "New Spain", Spanish ships also brought back new foods and plants to Europe. Tobacco, turkeys, cocoa, indigo, coffee beans, cochineal, potatoes, peppers, avocados, chocolate and corn were all previously unknown in Europe. In return, Spain introduced chickens, horses, mules, cattle, pigs and sheep to South America. Tobacco, maize, potato and canoe are all Indian words. South American food, especially Mexican food, is popular all over the world these days. You may have eaten corn *tortilla* chips yourself. However, if you should ask for a *tortilla* in Spain, you're quite likely to get a slice of omelette, made with onions and potatoes.

Colonies

By 1550, the *conquistadores* had overcome shipwreck, disease, battles with Indians, tropical jungles and mountain ranges to establish new colonies. These were governed from Spain by the Council of the Indies, and new cities were founded. Do you know which countries Havana, Santiago, Quito, Lima, Bogotá and La Paz are the capitals of?

| | Spanish Empire | | Area unknown to Europeans in 1588 |
| | Area known to Europeans in 1588 | | |

Hernán Cortés was the greatest Spanish conqueror in the Americas. His military triumphs led to 300 years of Spanish domination of Mexico and Central America.

Conquistadores

The *conquistadores,* or conquerors, were the men who fought the Indians to win new territory for Spain. Between 1519 and 1521, with just a few hundred men, Hernán Cortés overthrew the Aztec Empire and claimed Mexico. The Aztec king, Montezuma, thought Cortés was Quetzalcóatl, an Aztec god. With cannons and horses, which the Aztecs had never seen, Cortés and his men slaughtered them. In 1532, Francisco Pizarro conquered the Incas in Peru in a similar fashion. By the end of the 16th century, 80% of the native population of Mexico and Peru had been killed or had died from disease or overwork.

Montezuma's dead body was paraded in front of the Aztecs.

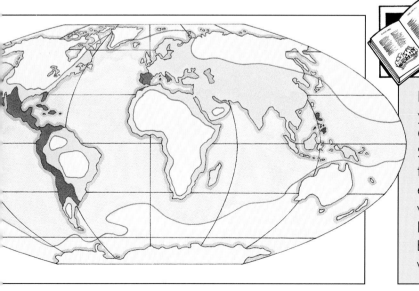

Names and places

Have a good look at a map of North and South America and locate as many Spanish place names as you can. They stretch from the tip of Chile deep into what is now the United States. Some of the names left by the first settlers are a little mysterious. For example, Las Vegas (the meadows), which is built in a desert; the Rio de la Plata (river of silver), which is muddy and brown; and Buenos Aires ("good airs"), which is hot and sticky.

THE COUNTRY

The Spanish countryside is extremely varied; the high central plateau, or *Meseta,* is surrounded almost entirely by mountains. Northern Spain is as green and wet as Ireland, while the south is hot and dry. The border with France is marked by the snow-capped Pyrenees, and the Canaries are volcanic islands off the coast of Northern Africa. Although the climate varies from region to region, Spain is the country with the most sunshine in Europe: 2,600 hours per year. One third of the country is covered with forest, and its most important rivers are the Duero, Tagus, Ebro and Guadalquivir.

Meseta

In the centre of Spain is a dry central plateau called the *Meseta.* It stands at an average height of 700m above sea level, and covers 210,000 sq km. The poor red or yellowish-brown soil is unsuitable for growing crops, but goats and sheep graze the highlands.

La Coruña ·   Bay of Biscay

· Santander

CANTABRIAN MOUNTAINS   NORTHERN MOUNTAINS   · San Sebastián   PYRENEES

Ebro   · Pamplona

EBRO BASIN

Duero   · Saragossa   Barcelona ·

Alagón   · Madrid   COASTAL PLAINS   BALEARIC ISLANDS   Minorca

Tagus   MESETA   · Toledo   Palma ·   Majorca

· Valencia   Ibiza

Zújar

Atlantic Ocean   · Alicante   Mediterranean Sea

GUADALQUIVIR BASIN

· Seville   · Granada

SIERRA NEVADA COASTAL PLAINS

· Málaga

Coast

Spain's coastline covers almost 4,000km ranging from the rugged coves of the Costa Brava to the sandy beaches of the Costa del Sol and the wild Atlantic coast around Finisterre, which means the end of the world.

Mountains

Winter sports are popular in Spain, especially in the Pyrenees. The highest point on the peninsula is the Mulhacén at 3,478m. The highest mountain in Spain is Mt Teide on Tenerife at 3,718m.

Regions

People in Spain are very proud of their own regions, and often identify more with the region than with the country as a whole. In recognition of this, each region has its own elected government. Some regions even have their own police force. Many regions are keen to have more power and less interference from central government, while some people would like to see their regions made totally independent from the national government of Spain.

1. Catalonia
2. Valencia
3. Castilla-La Mancha
4. Murcia
5. Andalusia
6. Extremadura
7. Madrid
8. Castilla & León
9. Galicia
10. Asturias
11. Cantabria
12. La Rioja
13. Basque Country
14. Navarra
15. Aragón
16. Balearic Islands
17. Canary Islands

Large areas of Spain are so arid, mountainous or remote that they are virtually uninhabitable. This makes them ideal for wildlife. Bears, wolves and the rare Spanish ibex still survive in the Pyrenees and mountain areas.

Doñana

Doñana, in the province of Huelva, is one of Europe's most important wetlands. It covers 700km^2 of mud flats, sand dunes and lagoons, where the river Guadalquivir passes into the Atlantic. Doñana is home to deer, wild boar, mongoose and lynx, eagles, kites, spoonbills and herons, and is the winter home of thousands of types of migratory bird. It is Spain's largest national park.

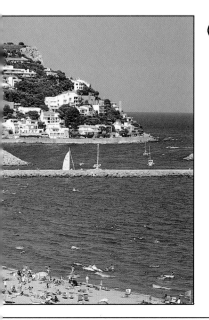

The Alcázar

Spain is dotted with more than 3,000 castles, evidence of centuries of invasions and regional warfare. Many have the name *Alcázar* from the Arabic word for fortress or castle. One of the most famous, in Segovia, is not as ancient as it looks, however. Started by the Moors in the 12th century and rebuilt in the Middle Ages, it was the fortified palace of the kings of Castile. It was destroyed by fire in 1862, and was then rebuilt in the style of a German Rhineland castle with ravens around its walls.

TOWNS AND CITIES

Madrid (population about 3,000,000) and Barcelona (about 1,500,000) are the biggest cities in Spain. Valencia, Bilbao, Seville, Saragossa and Málaga also have populations of over half a million. Spanish cities often have an old centre, with narrow streets around a *plaza mayor* (central square), mixed with modern apartment blocks and offices. In 1930, only 25% of Spain's population was urban. Now, 80% of Spaniards live in cities and towns, many in sprawling suburbs. Public transport in Spain is amongst the cheapest in Europe.

La Coruña · Vigo · Orense · Gijón · Oviedo · San Sebastian · Santander · Bilbao · León · Pamplona · Burgos · Logroño · Girona · Valladolid · Saragossa · Lleida · Barcelona · Salamanca · Madrid · Palma · Badajóz · Valencia · Córdoba · Albacete · Seville · Jaén · Alicante · Murcia · Granada · Jerez · Málaga

White houses

A typical image of the Andalusian *pueblos* (villages) is a jumble of white houses running along narrow streets. Many centuries ago, these houses were brightly coloured, but it was thought that painting them white helped resist the spread of plague.

Markets

Spaniards do a lot of shopping at markets, for food, clothes and many other things. Some markets are permanent, others are for just one day a week. Fresh food is essential in the Mediterranean diet, and the market place is always full of fresh fruit and vegetables, fish and meat. Whatever they sell, markets are always colourful, noisy and bustling. The Rastro flea market in Madrid fills dozens of streets on Sunday mornings, and crowds of people come out to wander amongst stalls selling everything under the sun.

Gaudí and Barcelona

Barcelona is often described as the most modern city in Spain. One reason for this is its architecture. Its most famous architect was Antonio Gaudí (1852-1926). Born into a family of iron workers, he became an architect in 1878.

He combined his metal working background and his observations of nature to build some of the world's most fantastic structures. Almost all his buildings are in and around Barcelona, and the most famous is the Sagrada Familia, a cathedral started in 1884 which is still being built today.

Traffic

The narrow streets in the centre of most Spanish cities were built with horses in mind rather than cars. As Spain has a high level of car ownership, many cities now suffer from terrible traffic and pollution problems. Some cities have closed their centres to cars altogether. The problem is so desperate that Spaniards often park anywhere. In some cities, it costs almost as much to buy a permanent parking space as it does to buy a small flat!

Religious aspirations

Most Spaniards are Catholics, and are baptised, married and buried within the Church. Attendance is falling though, and the Church has less influence on everyday life today than it did only twenty years ago. Nevertheless, many people participate in religious festivals. Spain has many beautiful cathedrals, like the ones at Burgos, León and Toledo, although many relics were destroyed in the Civil War. Many cathedral spires and bell towers are home to storks, which return to the same nest every year after wintering in Africa.

15

MADRID

Madrid, at 640m above sea level, is Europe's highest capital, and one of the hottest. Philip III made it the official capital in 1607, simply because it lay almost in the exact centre of the country. There was no military or economic reason for its choice, although previous kings had found its climate good for bad cases of gout. It is Spain's political and financial centre. The symbol of Madrid is a bear shaking a berry tree. It has a population of over 3 million and *Madrileños* (people from Madrid) like to stay up late into the night.

Puerta del Sol

In the centre of Madrid is the Puerta del Sol, where a gate *(puerta)* to the city once stood. This is *kilometre zero*; the centre of Spain, or the point from which all distances from the capital are measured. Madrid also has many large parks, such as the Retiro and the Casa del Campo, which were once royal hunting grounds. Modern Madrid stretches northward along a wide, tree-lined avenue. A small river flows through the city, called the Manzanares.

Plaza Mayor

This early 17th century square is Madrid's finest architectural feature. These days it is full of outdoor bars and cafés, where people sit talking late into the hot summer nights, but at one time heretics (religious rebels) were condemned to be burnt at the stake here, common criminals were executed and bullfights were held by nobles on horseback right up until the end of the 19th century.

The royal residence

The royal family live in the modest Palacio de la Zarzuela on the edge of Madrid. Built in the early 17th century as a hunting lodge, it was attacked by Napoleonic invaders, and by the 1950s it stood in ruins. It was renovated as the official residence for the then Prince Juan Carlos, who moved in during the 1960s. It is comfortable and modern, and without the luxury and size normally associated with royal palaces like El Escorial (an enormous rectangular palace, northwest of Madrid) and the Palacio Real with its 2,800 rooms and 23 courtyards (see page 21). It is also perhaps the only royal residence to be solar powered!

The Prado

The Prado was built as a museum of natural history, but it is now one of the greatest art galleries in the world. It was opened to the public in 1819, and the collection has remained virtually unchanged ever since. With over 3,000 paintings, pride of place goes to the Spanish masters Goya and Velázquez, whose bronze figures guard the door. It also contains important works by non-Spanish artists such as Brueghel, Rubens, Raphael, Titian and Hieronymous Bosch, amongst others.

New Year's Eve

On New Year's Eve in the Puerta del Sol, everybody tries to eat twelve grapes as the clock strikes midnight, one after each chime.

Bullfighting

One of Spain's most important bullrings, Las Ventas, is in Madrid. Bullfighting may date back to Roman or even Greek times, but the modern form of fighting the bull on foot, rather than horseback, dates from the 18th century. Bullfighting is a money-spinning industry, and leading *matadors* (men who fight the bulls) are rich and famous. Bullfights are often held to celebrate a town's *fiesta*. A good performance by a *matador* may be rewarded by giving him one or both of the bull's ears, or even the tail in exceptional circumstances.

Don Quixote

Miguel de Cervantes Saavedra (1547-1616) published his famous novel *Don Quixote* in 1605 (part I) and 1615 (part II). It is arguably the first modern novel and satirises stories of chivalry, as the slightly batty Don Quixote and his long-suffering servant Sancho Panza wander around Spain in search of adventure.

RURAL SPAIN

Less than a sixth of all Spanish people live in villages. The steady migration, especially of young people, to the towns and cities has left many villages deserted. As a result, huge areas of Spain have only a tiny population. Those that remain in the countryside make a living from agriculture, keeping livestock or both. Villages are normally built around a square, where the villagers can gather in the evenings to chat and have a drink.

Jornaleros
In spite of huge economic strides taken in the last few decades, Spain still has pockets of extreme poverty. Amongst the poorest are the *jornaleros*. These are agricultural workers hired by the day. They try to earn enough during the planting and picking seasons to sustain them throughout the year, and often travel around the country to follow the harvest.

Rural girls in traditional dress

Water
Water is a precious commodity, especially in central and southern Spain, where there are frequent droughts. Extensive dams, reservoirs and irrigation systems have been built, although some remote farms still use water courses built by the Arabs centuries ago. The Arabs turned barren regions into rich agricultural lands, and introduced rice and sugar cane to Spain. Due to erosion, changes in the climate and poor land management, some parts of Spain are now more like a desert.

La Mancha farmer from south-eastern Spain

High unemployment and rising prices have made it hard to make a living from the country, and much of the rural population has drifted towards the cities. People from central and north-western Spain tend to move towards Madrid, while those from the south and east often favour Barcelona. As a result, many villages, especially in central Spain, are now ghost towns.

In some regions, the traditional farmer lives in a big house surrounded by his land, with room for all the family and space beneath the house for animals, harvested crops and feed. He is fast disappearing, however. In 1950, almost half the population worked on the land. Now, only about 8% do. Laws in some regions prevent farms from being divided after the owners have died.

Popular opera

The *zarzuela* is a Spanish musical play which also includes spoken sections, songs, choruses and dances. It began in the 17th century as entertainment for aristocrats, full of heroes and mythology. It was revived in the mid-19th century, and shows scenes from everyday life. Nowadays, it includes folk music, dance and improvisation, and is still popular. Folk singing and dancing have long been popular in Spain, and the people of each region have their own songs and dances. Musicians provide accompaniment on castanets, guitars and tambourines.

Andalusian school of equestrianism

Andalusia has a long and proud tradition of horsemanship, and horses are still a part of rural life in the south. Spanish Arabian horses are raised on large estates in Andalusia and are internationally admired. At the Andalusian School of Equestrian Arts in Jerez, these elegant animals can be seen displaying the same discipline and sophistication as the horses of the Spanish Riding School in Vienna.

Isaac Newton Observatory

The Isaac Newton Observatory stands on the side of Spain's highest mountain, the Teide on the island of Tenerife. As Spain has so much sunshine, and the Canaries have such a stable climate, it is the ideal site for this international solar observatory. The futuristic white design helps protect the powerful telescopes from the strange effects caused by the ground warming up.

The mountains on Tenerife provide a perfect site for an observatory.

ORGANISATION

Spain is a constitutional monarchy, which means that it has a king as the head of state and a written constitution. The constitution describes the principles by which the country is to be governed, the institutions that will run the country and their responsibilities. The composition of Parliament is decided by general elections, which must be held at least every four years. The largest party then forms a government, which is led by a president. Spain's constitution was accepted in 1978, three years after the death of Franco.

Regions

Each one of the 17 regions of Spain is called a *Communidad Autónoma*, meaning autonomous community. All have their own elected regional government. They govern independently of the national government, as long as they do not go against Spain's interests as a whole. Some regional parties are also represented in the national Parliament. Towns and cities are run by the *ayuntamiento*, or town council, which is led by an elected *alcalde* or mayor. Even the smallest villages have an *alcalde*. The king is Spain's head of state. He does not have a direct role in the operations of government, but he represents the country at important diplomatic and ceremonial affairs.

King Juan Carlos and his wife Sofia represent Spain at official functions.

February 23 Coup

On February 23, 1981, Civil Guard Colonel Antonio Tejero, burst into Parliament brandishing a pistol. He fired shots into the ceiling and held the members hostage for 24 hours. He threatened to return Spain to the dark days of dictatorship. Some of the armed forces followed his lead, and tanks rolled through the streets of Valencia. The king intervened swiftly with an appearance on television, and ensured that the majority of the armed forces remained loyal to him. The problem was rapidly defused without casualties, and the ringleaders were imprisoned.

Currency

Since 1868 the unit of currency in Spain has been the *peseta*. However with the arrival of the euro as of 2002 the peseta is abolished. Some people still prefer to do their calculations in *duros*. A duro is a five peseta coin. Most Spanish coins bear an image of the king, while the 25 peseta piece has a hole in the middle. The highest denomination note is worth 10,000 pesetas. If five pesetas equals a duro, how many duros does it take to make 10,000 pesetas?

The Spanish Parliament

The Spanish Parliament building is called the Palacio de Las Cortes (built in 1850). It is one of the smallest in Europe. There are two houses, the Congress of Deputies and the Senate. The president is named by the king on the recommendation of the majority party and is assisted by a Council of Ministers. There are 350 members of Parliament, called *diputados*.

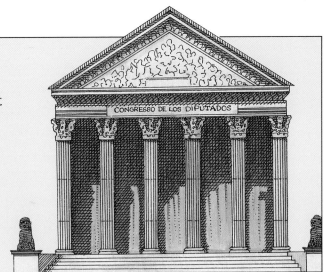

The Palacio Real (above) was built as the royal residence by Philip V in 1738, although it was last inhabited by Alfonso XIII and is now only used for important state occasions. Philip's original plan was for a much grander palace, but his wife convinced him that 2,800 rooms were probably quite enough!

Legal system

The Spanish legal system is like a pyramid, with the Supreme Court at the top, and more than 500 petty courts, or *juzgados* at the bottom. The king names the president of the Supreme Court. The Policía Nacional deals with crime in urban areas. The Guardia Civil guards Spain's ports, frontiers, coastlines and jails.

Armed forces

The army, navy and air force depend on the Ministry of Defence. The king is the commander-in-chief of the armed forces. Spain also has a foreign legion. It is compulsory for all Spanish men, except those exempt by law, to do a year of military service, or eighteen months of work which is beneficial to society. *La mili,* as it is known, is now widely resented by many young Spaniards. Anyone who refuses, however, may be sent to prison.

EDUCATION AND LEISURE

Education and leisure are important parts of life in Spain. Children aged between six and sixteen must attend school, and around 50% stay on to prepare for university. The fine weather makes it possible to spend a lot of time out of doors, and at weekends, traffic streams out of the cities to the beaches and mountains. In August, the traditional holiday month, the big towns seem deserted. Spaniards usually have four weeks holiday a year, but there are also 13 bank holidays, and when these fall on a Tuesday or a Thursday, many people turn them into a long weekend.

Compulsory schooling starts at six, although many children attend pre-school from the age of two. Children study eight years of Basic General Education, three years of *bachillerato*, and one year of university preparation. Salamanca University is one of the oldest in Europe. If children fail their annual exams, they may have to repeat the whole year. Spain has about 30 universities.

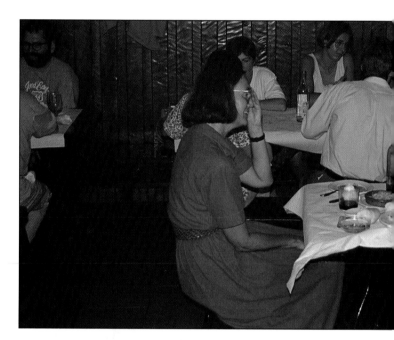

Fiestas

Fiestas (festivals) are like bank holidays, and Spain has lots of them. A *fiesta* may be in honour of a saint, mark an important religious occasion, or commemorate an important battle. They are often celebrated with lots of music, eating, drinking and fireworks. Some attract visitors from all over the world, such as the Fallas of Valencia, where enormous papier-mâché figures are burnt, the April Fair in Seville and San Fermín in Pamplona, where the night's revelry ends with people running through the streets in front of bulls being driven to the bull-ring.

Tapas

Lunch in Spain is often not until 3 o'clock, and dinner can be as late as 11 o'clock, so people keep their hunger at bay in bars and cafes with *tapas,* or small snacks. They may be seafood, omelette, salads, potatoes or even pig's ear. It is never difficult to find a bar either because there are more in Spain than any other EU country.

Lotteries

The Spaniards are great gamblers, and lotteries are big business in Spain. There are many different types of lotteries, but the most famous is *El Gordo*, which means "the fat one". Held just before Christmas, these lotteries can make whole villages or neighbourhoods rich overnight!

Soccer, basketball, cycling and tennis are the most popular sports in Spain. Spanish soccer club sides have performed very well in European competitions in recent years. Real Madrid beat fellow countrymen Valencia to win the UEFA Champions League Final in 2000. In tennis, both Arantxa Sanchez Vicario and Sergi Bruguera have won Grand Slam titles.

Opera

Spain has produced a lot of famous opera singers. The tenors, Placido Domingo, José María Carreras, Alfredo Kraus and the sopranos Montserrat Caballé and Victoria de los Angeles all perform at the world's most important opera houses. The Liceu opera house in Barcelona is one of Europe's finest. Opened in 1847, the stage is one of the largest in Europe, and about 15 opera productions are presented here each year. The neo-classical Opera House in Madrid was closed under Franco, but opened again in 1991.

Placido Domingo

José María Carreras

Monserrat Caballé

AGRICULTURE AND FOOD

Spain's agriculture varies with its climate and soil. It produces citrus fruit, apples, pears, figs, almonds, peaches, apricots, olives, grapes, barley, sugar beet, wheat and potatoes. Pastures make up one fifth of the land and forests one third, but fewer than 10% of the population are involved in agriculture, forestry or fishing. Spain is one of western Europe's largest agricultural producers, with 20 million hectares of arable land, although nearly half its total soil is barren or unproductive. Spain is one of the world's leading producers of cork, lemons, oranges, olives and wine. Bananas are grown in the Canary Islands.

Spaniards enjoy seafood, which is inexpensive and plentiful. Spanish favourites include squid, crab, sardines and fried baby eels.

Oranges

Spain produces million tonnes of oranges annually, which makes it the fourth most important producer after Brazil, the United States and Mexico. An orange tree can bear fruit for 80 years or more. The orange crop comes mainly from southern and eastern Spain.

Olives

Spain produces over million tonnes of olives per year. 90% is turned into olive oil, a key ingredient in Mediterranean cooking.

Livestock

Cattle are kept mainly in the north of Spain, and pigs are kept all over. Spain also has one of Europe's largest sheep and goat populations. Goats are mainly found in the south and the islands. Other important animals are beef and dairy cattle and poultry.

Foods

Tortilla, *paella* and *gazpacho* are some of the most popular dishes in Spain. A Spanish *tortilla* is an omelette made with eggs and potatoes; *paella* is made with rice flavoured with saffron and seafood, chicken, rabbit or other meats; and *gazpacho* is a cold soup made with tomatoes, onions, cucumbers and oil. A Spanish meal usually has two courses, a dessert and lots of bread and wine.

Paella

Fishing

Although the seas around Spain have been severely overfished, they are still productive, especially in cod, tuna and sardines. Spain has a fishing fleet of around 17,000 ships.

Wines and sherry

The Romans first brought grapes to Spain, and now, 2000 years later, Spain is an important wine producer. Most regions in Spain produce wine, but the most famous is *La Rioja*. Catalonia makes a champagne-like drink called *cava*. The name "sherry" comes from Jerez, the province where that drink is produced. Sherry's special flavour comes from the type of grapes, the type of soil and the fermenting process, in which a little air is allowed in to create a mildew-like growth. Brandy is also added, killing the yeast before all the sugar turns to alcohol.

Drinking wine from a leather bottle called a *porrón*

Market places

Every town, however small, has its market place, which is often purpose-built. Markets are usually tall, airy and quite old, with the sun streaming in through skylights, making them seem like cathedrals. The market is often decorated in wrought iron or ceramics with images of fruit and vegetables, fish or seafood to show agricultural wealth. The San Miguel Market in Madrid is enclosed in a lacy turn-of-the century ironwork building.

Oranges Pine cones Crabs
Flowers
Scallops

Hórreos

Hórreos are traditional grain stores that are mainly found in north-western Spain (Galicia). They stand on stilts a metre high to keep out rats and other pests. They are made of stone or wood, and the gap between the *hórreo* and the steps leading up to it is wide enough to stop animals crossing.

INDUSTRY AND EXPORT

Spain has never been one of Europe's leading industrial nations, but it has developed rapidly since the 1960s. It is an important manufacturer of chemicals, machine tools and motors. Heavy industry in Spain is concentrated largely around Barcelona and the Basque country. The Barcelona area manufactures cotton, woollen textiles and shoes. Cars are made by the Seat company. The national airline is called Iberia, and the railway company is called Renfe, which operates one of the world's fastest trains, called the AVE, between Madrid and Seville.

Resources

Spain has a wide variety of mineral resources, and although it led Europe in mineral production at the end of the last century, it only has small deposits of most minerals. It is one of the world's leading producers of mercury, and its next most important minerals are coal, iron ore, pyrite, titanium and uranium. It also produces copper, lead, potash, salt and zinc. Spain is heavily dependent on imported petrol. Its main mineral resource is the high-grade iron ore found in the Cantabrian Mountains.

□ Zinc		● Iron	
▨ Magnesium		● Coal	
▲ Potash		◐ Titanium	
△ Lead		◯ Tin	
▲ Copper		□ Manganese	
▲ Uranium		▨ Mercury	

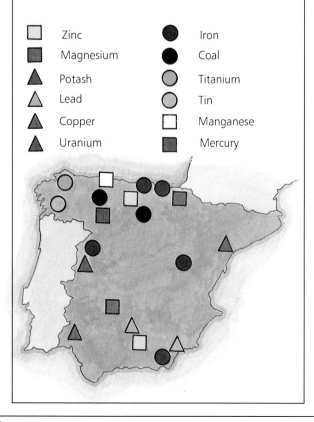

Industrial centres

Madrid is the centre of finance, banking and insurance in Spain. Barcelona is more commercial and industrial, with many chemical and plastics plants. Its textile manufacturers are concentrated along the Llobregat river. Bilbao is another hub of heavy industry, although its steel and shipbuilding industries have been hit hard in recent years and are in decline. Both Bilbao and Barcelona are major seaports.

Pottery and porcelain

Faience pottery is a type of tin-glazed earthenware which is made in France, Germany and Scandinavia, as well as Spain. It was originally developed in Moorish Spain and spread around Europe. Little faience pottery was produced after the early 19th century because of the popularity of creamware and porcelain. Lladró porcelain is produced in Valencia. Lladró figures have become collectable pieces worldwide.

IBERIA

Iberia Air Lines is government-owned and flies throughout Spain, to North and South America, and to many western European cities. It was founded in 1927 to carry passengers, goods and mail. During the summer, the airport at Palma, Mallorca, is one of the busiest in the world.

AVE

In order to link Madrid with Seville in time for the 1992 Expo, new track was laid and the high-speed train, called the AVE, was bought from France. The AVE can travel at speeds of up to 300 kph. Connections with the rest of Europe are not so easy, however, as fear of invasion caused Spain to construct its railways using a different gauge (track width).

Toledo steel

Toledo was a major city in old Spain and was written about as early as the 1st century BC. It was a great medieval centre for the study of alchemy (the search for a formula to make gold from other metals), and as the province is rich in iron ore, it was an important centre of steel production and the manufacture of daggers, swords and armour.

Craftwork

Spain is also famous for its craftwork – fine leather goods from Cordoba, lace from Galicia, delicate carpentry from Granada, jewellery from Toledo, rugs from the Las Alpujarras region north of Málaga and baskets from the Basque Country. Ceramic plates, pottery and colourful tiles are made in various regions of Spain, but especially around Valencia. Painted tiles called *azulejos* were brought to Spain by the Moors.

TODAY AND TOMORROW

Following years of dictatorship, Spain has successfully modernised at a pace which has taken other countries decades. Despite the new cars, elegant shops and fashionable clothes, poverty and unemployment remains widespread. Internationally, Spain is ideally placed as Europe's intermediary with North Africa and South America, and it participates in the summits of Spanish- and Portuguese-speaking countries. Spain is confident that it can compete in the new Europe, and its combination of sunshine, friendliness and curious customs continues to make it a popular place to visit.

EU

The European Union was founded in 1950 (as the European Economic Community) to promote agriculture, trade and industry amongst its members. Spain joined in 1986, after long negotiations. As one of the poorer European countries, Spain receives large injections of EU money for development.

UN

The United Nations (UN) is an international organisation set up after World War II in an attempt to help maintain the peace and stability of its members. It sends "peace keeping forces" to many trouble spots around the world. Spanish soldiers have participated in these missions.

ESA

Spain is a member of the European Space Agency. There is a ground station for satellites at Villafranca Del Castillo.

NATO

The North Atlantic Treaty Organisation (NATO) was founded in 1949 between the USA and a number of European countries. Spain became a member in 1982.

Basque separatism

The Basque country is the area around the Bay of Biscay at the western end of the Pyrenees, including a chunk of south-western France. Some Basques have long felt that their country should not be a part of Spain and have fought for independence since the unification of Spain in the 15th century. Although the Basque country was granted a degree of autonomy (self-government) in 1978, it did not satisfy more militant separatists, such as the terrorist organisation ETA.

Destination Spain

Tourism in Spain has grown from half a million visitors in 1960 to 72 million in 1999, which is more tourists than residents. While a key part of the Spanish economy, the rapid growth in tourism has also caused overdevelopment, overcrowding and the construction of horrible buildings at coastal resorts. The Spanish government has attempted to halt this explosion by demolishing illegally built hotels and apartments, and aiming instead for higher quality tourism.

Women in society

In the last twenty years or so, the position of women in Spanish society has changed drastically. In the past, it was not unusual for women to have enormous families and to stay at home to look after them. The birth rate has fallen rapidly in recent years to between one and two children per family, and the proportion of working women rose from 32% in 1982 to 48% in 1991. Under Franco's dictatorship, women needed their husband's permission to take a job or to travel within the country. Now they have a lot more freedom. The number of working women, however, is still below the EU average.

Expo and Olympics

Spain achieved international recognition in 1992 by staging two global events: the Barcelona Olympics and the Expo in Seville. The Expo was a six-month international fair with pavilions representing almost every country in the world. Expo finished on the 12th October, the day chosen to celebrate *Día de la hispanidad* (Spanish day) in all Spanish-speaking countries. With the Olympics, Barcelona became the centre of the world's attention for a fortnight, and Spain won 13 gold medals, a record for them.

Spain is a country with its sights fixed firmly on the future. Economic growth over recent years has meant that Spanish people enjoy a higher standard of living than ever before. Spain is also keen to play a greater role in European affairs, but it remains proud and protective of its traditions and culture.

FACTS AND FIGURES

Name: Reino de España (Kingdom of Spain)

Capital and largest city: Madrid (pop 3,012,000)

National anthem: *Marcha Real* ("The Royal March")

Currency: As of 2002, the euro, previously the *Peseta*

Population: 39,371,000

Official language: Spanish. Catalan, Galician and Basque are official second languages in provinces where they are widely spoken.

Population density: 78 persons per sq km

Distribution: 80% urban

Ethnic groups: Spanish 98%

Religion: Roman Catholic 67%, Muslim 1%, Protestant 1%, other 31%.

Area: 504,750km^2. Max distance, east-west 1,040km; north-south 880km

Highest mountain: Pico de Teide, 3,707m

Coastline: 3,774km

AVERAGE ANNUAL RAINFALL

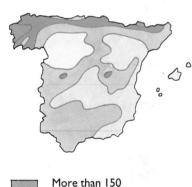

	More than 150
	100 to 150
	50-100
	Less than 50
	Centimetres

AVERAGE JANUARY TEMPERATURES

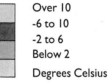

	Over 10
	-6 to 10
	-2 to 6
	Below 2
	Degrees Celsius

AVERAGE JULY TEMPERATURES

	Above 24
	20-24
	16-20
	Below 16
	Degrees Celsius

Main rivers: Tagus and Duero (both flow into Portugal then the Atlantic), Guadalquivir (flows into Atlantic in the south), Ebro (flows into Mediterranean Sea).

Climate: Northern Spain has mild summers, cool winters and plenty of rainfall all year. Rest of Spain has a Mediterranean climate with hot, dry summers and mild, moist winters.

Physical features: Extreme north is divided from the rest of Spain by Cantabrian and Galician mountains. Most of Spain is plateau. The Pyrenees and the Sierra Nevada are the most notable mountain ranges.

Borders: The Pyrenees Mountains form the border with France in the north. In the west, Spain's border is with Portugal.

AGRICULTURE

Crop production
Barley, sugar beets, wheat, corn, grapes, potatoes, olives and fruit.

Livestock
Sheep, pigs, cattle and goats.

Land use
Forests and woodland 32%, arable land 30%, permanent pastures 21%, permanent crops 9%, other 8%.

MINERAL RESOURCES

Spain is poor in natural resources. It lacks many important industrial raw materials.

INDUSTRY

Textiles and clothing (including footwear), food and beverages (see wine production, below), metals and metal manufacture, chemicals, shipbuilding, automobiles, machine tools.

TOURISM

Receipts: (1996)
US$25,701 million

Expenditure: (1996)
US$4,540 million

Imports
Machinery 12%, energy products 9% (most of which is crude petroleum), transportation equipment 8%, agricultural products 8%.

Major import sources:
France 18%, Germany 15%, Italy 10%, UK 8%.

Spain spends around US$137.5 billion per year on imports.

Exports
Transport equipment 20%, agricultural products 13%, machinery 8%.

Major export destinations:
France 20%, Germany 15%, Italy 9%, UK 8%.

Annually, Spain receives some US$112.3 billion from exports.

ELECTRICITY

Production by source:

Fossil fuels	48.23%
Nuclear	31.23%
Hydroelectric	19.16%
Other	1.38%

ECONOMY

The GDP (gross domestic product) is the amount of goods and services produced within a country. By dividing the GDP by the population a *per capita* result is reached.

Figures shown are the GDP per capita in the year 1997. (GDPs are shown in US dollars).

Spain	13,412
USA	28,789
Germany	25,468
Belgium	23,948
Netherlands	23,270
UK	21,927
Italy	19,962

Spain is famous for its wine industry and it exports millions of bottles of wine every year. The country as a whole produces around 4.5 million tonnes of grapes annually.

FAMOUS FACES

WRITERS

Miguel de Cervantes Saavedra (1547-1616). See pages 5 and 15.

Lope Felix de Vega Carpio (1562-1635) wrote as many as 1,500 plays, as well as ballads and poems. He was also a soldier and officer of the Inquisition, and served in the Spanish Armada in 1588.

Pedro Calderón de la Barca (1600-1681) was a poet and playwright. He also served for many years as a soldier and entered the priesthood. He wrote a lot of plays for the court, church and public theatres.

José Echegaray y Eizaguirre (1833-1916) was a mathematics teacher, physics professor, government minister and dramatist, and won the Nobel prize for literature in 1904. His most famous work was *The Great Galeoto* (1881).

Frederico García Lorca (1899-1936, right). Lorca was a poet and playwright. See page 9.

Miguel de Unamuno (1864-1936, left). Unamuno was a philosophical essayist, poet, novelist and dramatist. His best known work is *The Tragic Sense of Life* (1913).

Jacinto Benavente (1866-1954) wrote many plays, poems and short stories, and was awarded the Nobel prize for literature in 1922.

ARTISTS

El Greco (1541-1614, right). El Greco's real name was Domenico Theotocopoulos. See page 7.

Francisco Zurbarán (1598-1662) was a city painter and court painter to Philip IV. He specialised in pictures of saints.

Diego de Silva y Velázquez (1599-1660). See page 7.

Francisco José de Goya y Lucientes: (1746-1828, left) was court painter to Charles IV. He painted the royal family in a very unflattering way. He also produced many jolly scenes of Madrid life and "the black paintings", a series of dark and macabre pictures.

Pablo Picasso (1881-1973, right). Picasso was perhaps the most famous 20th century artist. Besides many innovative paintings, Picasso also sculpted and produced stage sets.

Joaquín Sorolla y Bastida (1863-1923) was a leading Spanish Impressionist known for his ability to paint light.

Joán Miró (1893-1983, above). Miró was a Catalan artist who was converted to Surrealism. His fantastic shapes suggest dream-like situations, and his work eventually became almost entirely abstract.

Salvador Dalí (1904-1989, right). A member of the Surrealist movement, Dali's most famous painting is *The Persistence of Memory*. He collaborated with film director Luis Buñuel on *Un Chien Andalou* (1928) and *L'Age d'Or* (1930).

MUSICIANS

Isaac Albéniz (1860-1909) was a Spanish composer and pianist and was one of the creators of a national style for Spanish music. His most famous composition, *Iberia* (1908), consists of four books of solo piano music. His orchestral works include *Spanish Rhapsody* (1887) and *Catalonia* (1899). From 1893 to 1900, he lived in Paris, where his music influenced the French composers Claude Debussy and Maurice Ravel. Albéniz was born in Camprodón in Catalonia and gave his first piano recital at the age of four. He was a respected concert pianist throughout his life.

Enrique Granados y Campiña (1868-1916) was a composer and pianist.

Manuel De Falla (1876-1946, right). De Falla is perhaps the most famous Spanish composer. He became known internationally with his ballet *The Three-Cornered Hat*. He settled in South America when the Civil War broke out.

Pablo Casals (1876-1973) was a cellist, conductor and composer. He founded the Barcelona Orchestra, which he conducted until the outbreak of the Civil War, when he left Spain and did not return. He composed choral and chamber works.

Andrés Segovia (1893-1987, right) was a superb guitarist. His revolutionary guitar technique enabled him to play a wide range of music. He gave his first recital at the age of 14. Many composers wrote works for him. By the 1920s, he was so well known, the French composer Roussel wrote a guitar piece called simply *Segovia*. Segovia taught the Australian-born John Williams and many other leading guitar players.

Montserrat Caballé (1933-). See page 23.

Placido Domingo (1941-) is a popular opera singer. He is a tenor and gained international praise for his performances in Italian operas. Domingo was born in Madrid, but moved to Mexico with his family in 1950. He made his opera debut in 1960 in Monterrey, Mexico. See page 23.

José Carreras (1946-). See page 23.

Joaquín Rodrigo (1901-1999) was a composer. He wrote a very popular work for the guitar called *Concierto de Aranjuez*. He also wrote a magnificent tribute to the guitarist Segovia, called *Fantasia para un Gentilhombre* (Fantasia for a Nobleman) based on themes by the 17th century guitarist Gaspar Sanz.

PIONEERS

Francisco Pizarro (1478-1541).
See page 11.

Hernán Cortés (1485-1547).
See page 11.

Fernando De Soto (1496-1542) assisted Pizarro in the conquest of Peru and conquered Florida. He was the first European to cross the Mississippi.

Francisco Vázquez de Coronado (1510-1554) was a *conquistador* and explorer in Mexico. He also led an expedition into what is now the United States and was the first European to see the Grand Canyon.

Christopher Columbus (1541-1506).
See page 10.

Santiago Ramón y Cajal (1852-1934) was a Spanish physician. His most famous work concentrated on the brain and nerves. He isolated the neuron and discovered how nerve impulses are transmitted to the brain. He was awarded the Nobel Prize for Medicine in 1906.

Dolores Ibarruri Gómez (1895-1989), also known as *La Pasionaria*. She helped found the Spanish Communist party in 1920 and encouraged the Spanish people to fight the fascists during the Civil War by saying, "It is better to die on your feet than to live on your knees". After decades in exile, she was re-elected to Parliament at the age of 81.

Nuria Espert (1935-) is an actress and stage director, and has appeared in plays all over the world. She has also directed plays and operas.

Felipe González (1942-) was first elected prime minister in 1982, and has since won four general elections as leader of the Spanish socialist party.

Pedro Almodóvar (1942-). Famous film director whose films have been successful worldwide. These include *Women on the Verge of a Nervous Breakdown*, *High Heels* and *All About My Mother*.

Spanish terms used in English

Spanish is a Romance language, which means it has its origins in Latin, the language of the Romans. As part of the English language is also of Romance origin, Spanish and English expressions sometimes coincide. There are a few Spanish words that have been absorbed by the English language:

arena	a big stadium – literally "sand".
canyon	a gorge (from *cañon*)
desperado	a bandit or desperate person
fiesta	a party or a day's holiday
liberal	a political attitude
matador	a bullfighter
parasol	an umbrella-shaped sunshade
plaza	a square
propaganda	information that is not necessarily true
siesta	an afternoon nap
vigilante	a guard
villa	detached house for holidays

INDEX